The Story of God
EXPLORING THE BIBLICAL NARRATIVE

D1411696

BEACON HILL PRESS
OF KANSAS CITY

Editor
Mike L. Wonch
Director of Curriculum
Merritt J. Nielson
Director of Editorial
Bonnie Perry
Writer
Michael Lodahl

All scripture quotations, unless otherwise indicated, are from the *New Revised Standard Version* (NRSV) of the Bible, copyright 1989 by the Division of Christian Education of the National Council of the Churches of Christ in the USA. Used by permission. All rights reserved.

All rights reserved. No part of this publication may be reproduced, stored in a retrieval system, or transmitted in any form or by any means—for example, electronic, photocopy, recording— without the prior written permission of the publisher. The only exception is brief quotations in printed reviews.

The internet addresses, email addresses, and phone numbers in this book are accurate at the time of publication. They are provided as a resource. Beacon Hill Press does not endorse them or vouch for their content or permanence.

Copyright 2014 by Beacon Hill Press of Kansas City

Beacon Hill Press of Kansas City
PO Box 419527
Kansas City, MO 64141
nph.com

ISBN: 978-0-8341-3351-8

Printed in the
United States of America

10 9 8 7 6 5 4 3 2 1

CONTENTS

To Scotty and Elizabeth Young:

Hopefully at least some of this is in Deuteronomy!

Telling the Story of God:

Scripture, Tradition, Reason and Experience

What is the Story of God? And how do we tell it?

There is this wonderful, mysterious story told in the gospel of Luke:

On the first Easter Sunday, in the day's waning hours, a pair of disheartened disciples trudged on the road from Jerusalem to Emmaus. In melancholy tones they mulled over what they had seen during the horrible weekend, "talking with each other about all these things that had happened" (Luke 24:14). They were trying to make some sense of Jesus' betrayal, arrest, suffering, and crucifixion; they were desperately seeking a way to comprehend their recent traumatic *experience*. In their own words to the Stranger who had joined them somewhat mysteriously on their painful journey, "we had hoped that he was the one to redeem Israel" (v. 21). But how could Israel's redeemer have met such a horrid fate? It made no sense to them; it was contrary to reason.

In this story from the *Scriptures*—a story with which, through the exercise of *reason*, I have chosen to begin this book—these disciples themselves were employing *reason* to try to interpret their *experiences* in Jerusalem over the weekend.

We should add that their hope in Jesus as Israel's redeemer had been fueled by certain *traditions* of interpreting the Hebrew *Scriptures*. They were reflecting one of the traditional Jewish beliefs about the messiah—a tradition clearly rooted in the Jewish people's long history of reading the Torah (Law) and the Prophets.

In the midst of their confusion and disappointment, we read that "Jesus himself came near and went with them" (v. 15)—but they did not recognize the Resurrected One. After listening to their litany of dashed hopes, the mysterious Stranger "interpreted to them the things about himself in all the scriptures . . . beginning with Moses and all the prophets" (v. 27). The

Resurrected Christ, inexplicably incognito, was giving them eyes to read their Scriptures in a radically new way. He did so, we should note, through the interchange of conversation, interpretation, teaching—the use of *reason*. He did not perform magic, but actually engaged them in reasoned discourse about how to rightly interpret Scripture.

But this story bears witness to far more than the employment of reason; after all, this unknown traveler was the resurrected Christ—not your everyday *experience*! Scholars note that in biblical writing, the use of a passive verb (such as "their eyes were kept from recognizing him" in verse 16) often denotes divine action. Somehow, it was God's will that they not yet recognize Jesus. There is, then, something exceedingly mysterious here, something elusive and transcendent. Their review of the scriptures was a religious *experience* par excellence. The living Christ walked alongside his reeling disciples in the midst of their disheartenment.

The nature of this dramatic experience becomes all the more evident when we recall how these disciples later described their stroll with the Stranger: "Were not our hearts burning within us while he was talking to us on the road, while he was opening the scriptures to us?" (v. 32). Their heartwarming *experience* included *rational* communication and argument through opening the *Scriptures*. Even so, it was not until Jesus took bread, gave thanks, broke it, and distributed it, reliving all those meals with his disciples, those feedings of the hungry multitudes, that final Passover meal, that "their eyes were opened, and they recognized him; and he vanished from their sight" (v. 31). The implication, again, is that God opened their eyes (cf. Acts 10:40). They realized they were in the company of the living Lord Jesus—and then he instantly vanished. This is surely a spiritual experience for the ages.

But Luke's account does not end there. The amazed pair raced back to Jerusalem to report their experience to the other disciples, especially how Jesus "had been made known to them in the breaking of the bread" (Luke 24:35). This story in the *Scriptures*, then, testifies to an *experience* of the risen Christ that would provide rich resources for the development of the *tradition* of the Lord's Supper, in which we too believe and expect that Jesus will be made known to us "in the breaking of the bread." By breaking that bread together, we are physically drawn into the story of living as disciples on the rough and tangled roads of life, striving to make sense of its hard realities, yet journeying in the very company of the living Christ. It is he who continues to open the Scriptures to us, and it is his resurrection presence that still sets hearts on fire.

The Wesleyan Quadrilateral

In the Church of England during the time of John Wesley (1703-1791), it was typical for theologians to acknowledge the importance of church *tradition* and human *reason* in rightly interpreting the *Scriptures*. Wesley certainly agreed with this, but he also cleared a significant place for spiritual *experience* (as well as experience in the more general sense). These four elements have become known as "the Wesleyan quadrilateral," and though the idea of the quadrilateral is sometimes misunderstood or misused, it certainly points us in an important and helpful direction. The story of the resurrected Christ and his disciples, which is found in the *Scriptures,* but which I also chose for a *reason* (that is, I didn't simply open up the Bible and point randomly to a verse on the page) helps us see how *Scripture*, *tradition*, *reason*, and *experience* are deeply intertwined.

While most of us will probably never have quite so dramatic an encounter with Christ as the discouraged disciples on the Emmaus Road, it remains true that all theological reflection—even the simplest reading of a biblical passage—involves all four of these elements to some extent or another. Thus, even if it is Wesleyans who tend to talk the most about the "the Wesleyan quadrilateral," it is inevitable that anyone who attempts to think carefully about his or her Christian faith will necessarily incorporate Scripture, tradition, reason, and experience.

An important point to be gained from these considerations is that the Bible never stands alone as it speaks to us. We must read it, and when we read we are also always interpreting—and every act of interpretation inevitably entails the use of reason. Reason, in turn, never stands alone either; the way we think about things is shaped and informed by a complex variety of traditions.

Reason and Tradition

To tell God's Story well, then, we need to recognize the important role that tradition plays in both our hearing and our telling. The traditions that surround and nurture us provide us with ways in which to think, and so also the lens through which we read, understand, and apply the Bible. Tradition is not only something we inherit, a body of accumulated interpretation of Scripture, but also something we may contribute to through preaching, teaching, praying, worshipping, writing, testifying, and simply living. (I am thinking of the wonderful saints of my home church whose lives influenced me so deeply during my teen years.) The tradition that has shaped you includes the sermons and Sunday School lessons you have heard or prepared, the hymns and other forms of worship in which you have participated with other believers over the years, the books and Bible commentaries you have browsed, and the pastors or other Christian leaders you have watched in the acts and virtues of day-to-day living (Heb. 13:7). Tradition is the inevitable reality of being limited, finite creatures living in history and within specific communities, including not only religious denominations but also the cultural, ethnic, and political dimensions of communal life. We are not absolutely determined by our traditions, but we (including our capacity for reasoning) are certainly deeply shaped by them.

Scripture and Experience

Further, we always open our Bibles with a rich stream of experience flowing into our work of interpretation. Given his strong convictions about the Holy Spirit "bearing witness with our spirit that we are children of God" (Rom. 8:16; see also Gal. 4:6) and his own "heart-warming" experience of Christ as a young man, it is not surprising that Wesley imparted to the Methodists (and later to the American holiness movement) a lively hope for experiencing the dynamic presence and activity of the Spirit in our hearts and churches. And while we need the Scriptures to shape our expectations about experiences with God, Wesley also believed that experience could in turn provide critical insights for interpreting the scriptures!

In one dramatic example, a critic asked Wesley what he would do if no one could find any actual human beings living up to the ideal of Christian perfection that Wesley preached. He replied that if that were actually the case, he would have to quit preaching it. But, his critic asked, didn't Wesley believe that his teaching was supported by Scripture? If it were scriptural, would it matter if no one actually lived up to it? Wesley responded thus: "If I were convinced that no one in England had attained what has been so clearly and strongly preached by such a number of preachers, in so many places, and for so long a time, I would be clearly convinced that we had all mistaken the meaning of those Scriptures."[1] If the interpretation of Scripture does

---

1. Wesley, John. *A Plain Account of Christian Perfection.* (Kansas City: Beacon Hill Press, 1966), p. 67.

not fit with what actually is the case as established through long and careful observation, said Wesley, then the interpretation is inadequate.

An even more important point regarding experience is that we need the living Jesus to be our companion and teacher on the rough road of life. Let us remember that the Risen Christ "interpreted to them the things about himself in all the scriptures" (v. 27). This is a critical theme in the Story of God—that Jesus is at the heart of that Story. We believe that God's ultimate and final revelation is Jesus himself, for "the Word became flesh and lived among us" (John 1:14; see also Hebrews 1:1-3). It is Jesus' life and ministry, words and works, death and resurrection all taken together that most fundamentally reveal to us who God is and what God is like.

Bodies and Sacraments

We should remember, too, that even though the disciples' hearts burned within them as Christ taught them about himself from the Hebrew Scriptures, it was not until Jesus actually broke bread with them that "their eyes were opened." It was in *the breaking of the bread* that God allowed Jesus to be recognized. We need the Scriptures, interpretation, teaching, and the guidance of the Spirit of Christ as we read, but we also need to encounter the living Christ sacramentally in the bread we break and the cup we share. "The cup of blessing that we bless, is it not a sharing the blood of Christ? The bread that we break, is it not a sharing in the body of Christ?" Paul asked the Corinthian church. "Because there is one bread, we who are many are one body, for we all partake of the one bread" (1 Cor. 10:16-17). We are not just thinking minds or even just feeling hearts; we are also bodies enfolded in a material world, created by God and deemed by God to be very good (Gen. 1:31). Through these material elements of the bread and the cup, the Story of God communicates to our bodies in a physical way.

Once more, I will employ reason in selecting and citing Scripture: we read earlier in the same letter to the Corinthians that "no one can lay any foundation other than the one that has been laid; that foundation is Jesus Christ" (1 Cor. 3:11). Just as it was God who opened the eyes of those two confused, worn, and forlorn disciples after their heart-wrenching weekend in Jerusalem, God laid Jesus as the foundation for Christian faith, life, and thought. May we pray for the same sort of eye-opening grace as we move into Chapter 2 of God's Story, in which we begin to think upon the doctrine of God as Creator of all things. As we do so, we will try to build faithfully upon the foundation that the Creator has in fact laid for us: the foundation of Jesus Christ, the crucified and living Lord whom we celebrate and encounter at his holy meal of the broken bread and the shared cup.

Reflect on this...

What are your thoughts and feelings after reading this chapter?

How has this chapter helped you better understand the Story of God?

In what ways are you involved in this part of God's Story today?

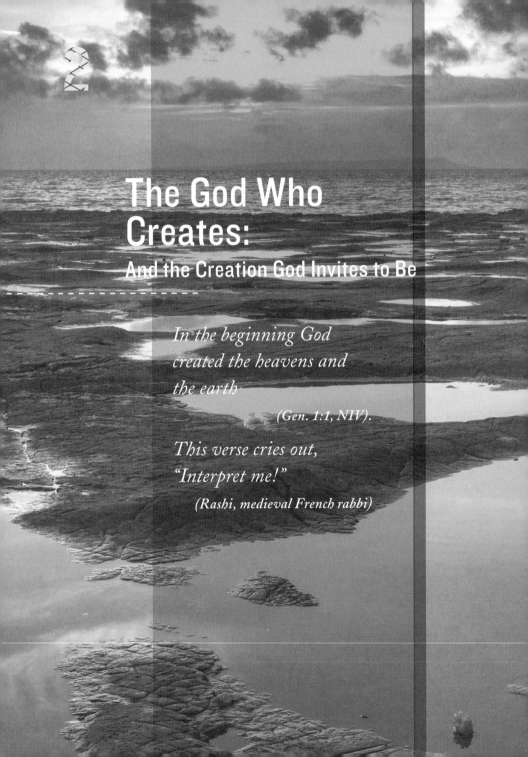

The God Who Creates:
And the Creation God Invites to Be

In the beginning God created the heavens and the earth

   (Gen. 1:1, NIV).

This verse cries out, "Interpret me!"

   (Rashi, medieval French rabbi)

Rashi was commenting on the opening verse in the Bible, but his wry observation is true of far more than that first verse! Every time we open our Bible to read, or hear the Scripture read, we are beckoned and bound to be interpreters. Jesus certainly recognized this. Once when a Jewish scholar asked him how to inherit eternal life, Jesus responded with a pair of his own questions: "What is written in the Law? How do you read it?" (Luke 10:26). And how *do* we? We cannot escape this task of interpretation, for indeed it is given to us by God.

But of course we are not simply interpreters. Interpretation goes both ways, for the Bible also interprets us. As we read and meditate upon its testimony and teachings about the God of creation and redemption, we discover that we are becoming incorporated into the Bible. In a profound sense, Scripture reads *us*, calling us to interpret ourselves from its perspective, to enter into its orbit, to be drawn into its story. When this happens, it is no longer a matter of trying to fit the Bible into our lives, but of trying to understand and live our lives in the light of the Bible's rich testimony to the God of Israel, the Father of our Lord Jesus Christ. Indeed, the Holy Spirit works to weave our lives as Christians into the very Story of God.

Everyone loves a good story. We naturally think of our lives as a story—with a beginning, important characters, a plot with twists, turns, and surprises, and often an anticipated ending that we hope will help make sense of it all. Most of us like hearing other folks' stories too, partly because they often shed new light upon our own.

Because we are tantalized by stories and tend to interpret our own lives accordingly, it is no surprise that the Bible corresponds beautifully to this narrative pattern. The Scriptures tell an overarching story that stretches from creation to the dawning of the age to come. It is our calling as Christians to proclaim and to live that story faithfully.

In this light, it is entirely fitting that Scripture bears witness to a God who speaks, and that God's speech calls the universe into being. In Genesis, it is the speaking of God, the meaningful arranging of divine words, that begins the story of all creation. In reading or hearing Scripture, we find ourselves invited into that story. "Why did God create the world?" a young Jewish student asked his rabbi. The reply? "Because God loves stories."

Creation in the Light of Redemption

The stories of the Bible, in fact, often intertwine and shed light upon each other. For example, many biblical scholars point out that the creation story in Genesis 1 is told in the light of the Jewish Exodus from Egypt; most obviously, the parting of the Red Sea resonates deeply with the parting of the waters above from the waters below in Genesis 1:6. Similarly, Psalm 74 brings images of creation and Exodus into convergence, like a double-exposure photo; God's act of creation is extolled as one of the great "deeds of deliverance" in which God "divided the sea" (74:12, 13). The logic of such an approach to creation would be, essentially, "The God who delivered us out of Egypt's bondage is also Creator of heaven and earth." In both events there is the powerful Spirit-breath of God "dividing" the waters, blowing back their threatening waves, so that a new creation might occur. In Exodus, it is the creation of a people before God, a people of identity and vocation; in Genesis, it is the creation of a world. In both cases, God's word is "Let there be"—let there be a real creation, a real people, a true "other" that is not God nor is it "under God's thumb."

Just as the Jewish understanding of creation is framed by a collective memory of the Exodus, so also we Christians interpret the creation of the world through our great story of deliverance, the gospel of Jesus Christ. John's Gospel, for example, tells us that the creative word (*logos*) that God spoke in creation is the same Word that joined with creation in the person of Jesus of Nazareth (1:1, 14). Similarly, Paul insists that "it is the God who said, 'Let light shine out of darkness,' who has shone in our hearts to give the light of the knowledge of the glory of God in the face of Jesus Christ" (2 Cor. 4:6). The point is that the early Christian community, living in the light of Christ's powerful redemption, saw even God's act of creation in that light. "He is the image of the invisible God, the firstborn of all creation. . . . He himself is before all things, and in him all things hold together" (Col. 1:15, 17).

Christ Reveals the Creator's Character

This has rich and profound implications for our understanding of God, of creation, and of the problem of evil. It means our Christian confession is that God's heart in the act of creation is a Christlike heart. The bold statement of 1 John—"God is love" (4:8, 16)—is not the result of theological speculation, but of Christ's self-giving on the cross. If Christ is at the center of the Christian doctrine of creation, then God's act of creation reflects the very self-giving, other-receiving love embodied in the Crucifixion. God's creative word is "Let there be," the word of a Love who shares being with all of us creatures! This Word of Love became flesh and dwelt among us, and he gave himself up for us. There is a cross in creation!

If indeed Christ on the cross is the decisive revelation of God the Creator, then divine power is not a ruling fist but an open, bleeding hand. This ought to challenge common ideas about divine omnipotence. The fact that Christ, the Word become flesh, was nailed to a cross by other men reveals a vulnerability on God's part, a humble willingness to suffer our shameful violence in the abuse of the very freedom he gave us.

But if the cross bespeaks God's willingness to suffer at the hands of the creature, the Resurrection reminds us that God is ultimately the victorious power. Paul's understanding of divine sovereignty was not that God determines every event in our lives like some master solitary chess player, but that God's love for us is the one indestructible power in the universe. Because God raised Jesus from the dead, Paul testified that "neither death, nor life, nor angels, nor rulers, nor things present, nor things to come, . . . nor anything else in all creation, will be able to separate us from the love of God in Christ Jesus our Lord" (Rom. 8:38-39).

Interpreting Genesis I with Saint Augustine

Jesus Christ is the ultimate revelation of the God of all creation. But as "the last Adam" or "the second man" (1 Cor. 15:45, 47) he is also the perfect unveiling of humanity. While all human beings are created in God's image, Jesus himself is "the image of the invisible God" (Col. 1:15). In his person, words and works, we see what God envisions for human life.

Saint Augustine of Hippo (354-430) understood this very well. In his classic work *Confessions*, we find that even in his time, Christians hotly contested how to interpret Genesis 1. Their disagreements are not the same as ours today, and need not detain us here. The critical thing is that Augustine responded to these debates by moving his readers toward Jesus. Drawing from Jesus' words in Matthew 22:36-40, he observed that, most fundamentally, human beings are created to love God with all their being (Deut. 6:5) and to love all neighbors as themselves (Lev. 19:18). We are made to receive God's love, to return God's love, and to share God's love.

Augustine then wisely notes Jesus' statement that "On these two commandments hang all the law and the prophets" (Matt. 22:40). He reminds us that the Law (Torah) includes Genesis, and thus includes the very passages of controversy. To put it simply, all of Genesis 1 "hangs on" the dual commandment of love for God and neighbor. This means that even the creation story hangs on these two great commands. Consequently, we ought to be reading Genesis 1 to discover what it is that God desires of our lives. On this basis Augustine made a crucial appeal to his readers, especially to those who disagreed with his interpretation of Genesis 1: "Do you not see how foolish it is to enter into mischievous arguments which are an offense against that very charity for the sake of which [Moses] wrote every one of the words that we are trying to explain?"[2]

We must keep in mind that Augustine was still grappling with the opening verses of Genesis and suggesting that they were written "for the sake of . . . charity," for the sake of calling us to greater love for God and all neighbors. To dispute over how to understand Genesis's opening chapter causes us to run the great risk of missing the very purpose of the text.

For Augustine, then, God's teaching is consistently aiming "to nourish love" in our lives and all relationships. Genesis 1 describes human beings as created in God's image, and now we have come to comprehend through Jesus Christ that *God is love.* Now we can see that to be created in God's image is to be created for love—to receive love, to share love. According to Augustine, this love for God and all neighbors is the very point of Genesis, including Genesis 1.

Godly Dominion

If we interpret Genesis 1 in this light, it will help us better understand our divine vocation to "be fruitful and multiply," to "fill the earth and subdue it," and to "have dominion over the fish of the sea and over the birds of the air

---

2. Saint Augustine of Hippo. *Confessions,* trans. R.S. Pine-Coffin. (New York, Penguin Books, 1961), 303.

and over every living thing that moves upon the earth" (Gen. 1:28). These tasks ought to be fulfilled in the energy and spirit of wholehearted love for the Creator of all these creatures. Earlier in the story, the Creator had already blessed these creatures of sea and sky with the invitation to "be fruitful and multiply" (1:22). Human beings were created to "image" God, to reflect the God who has been revealed as self-emptying love through Jesus Christ. Our dominion (from the Latin *dominus*, which means "lord") ought to imitate the kind of dominion we have seen in Jesus our Lord who, "knowing that the Father had given all things into his hands" (John 13:3), put those very hands to the humble task of washing his disciples' feet!

As we continue to grow in our understanding of how our actions in the present affect the world and resources that our children and grandchildren will inherit, God's calling to love all neighbors becomes a guiding principle for all who understand themselves to be "the new self, which is being renewed in knowledge according to the image of its Creator" through Jesus Christ (Col. 3:10). If "all of the law and the prophets hang on these two commands" of love for God and neighbor, then surely we are to read all of Scripture with an eye toward nourishing and nurturing greater, deeper and wider love for God and for all our neighbors. That includes our future neighbors with whom we share God's good creation.

Reflect on this...

What are your thoughts and feelings after reading this chapter?

How has this chapter helped you better understand the Story of God?

In what ways are you involved in this part of God's Story today?

3

The Tragedy of
God's Story:

The Doctrine of Sin

In the opening chapters of the Bible, one of the profound observations about human life is that we are deeply interconnected with one another. "No man is an island," wrote the poet John Donne, and surely that truth comes to life for us in Genesis. We read there of God's declaration that "It is not good that the man should be alone" (Gen. 2:18), which underscores the profoundly social dimension of human life. We truly do influence one another by what we say, think, and do, and simply by being ourselves in the company of others. This deep interconnection with one another is implied in the Christian doctrine of original sin.

Genesis also teaches that human disobedience toward God wields the power to corrupt and even destroy our relations with God, our neighbors, and the rest of creation. Ironically, it is precisely because we are relational and social beings that sin can exercise such power. Sin poisons the very relationships without which we and others cannot truly live.

The Story of Cain and Abel

Surely it is this relational situation of sin that is described in the story of Cain and Abel (Gen. 4). Here we encounter the rawest of human emotions laid bare: sibling rivalry giving way to jealousy, jealousy to hatred, hatred to violence and murder—and all of it followed by a casual and cavalier denial of the whole thing. Cain and Abel were brothers; they were kindred—but this kinship did not prevent sin from growing. In fact, it may have encouraged its spread.

I still remember hearing, many years ago, a Jewish scholar named Pinchas Peli use the story of Cain and Abel to shed light on how atrocities such as the Holocaust could occur. "Cain exercised his God-given freedom," said Peli, "and obliterated one-fourth of the human race . . . while God stood by and did nothing."

But is it true that God did nothing? Peli's thinking seemed to reflect a traditional rabbinic idea that essentially put these words into Cain's mouth: "You, God, are the Almighty! You come here and ask me where Abel is, when you know full well that you could have stopped me. Where were you when I killed my own brother? You didn't lift a finger! So maybe it's your fault that Abel is dead!"

That might sound familiar. There is something frightening about the power that God has entrusted to us. It would be preferable, in some ways, to be able to forfeit this power and hope that God will pull all the strings. But would we really desire that God interrupt or cancel our freedom? Without freedom, could we love?

Of course, Genesis 4 does not report that "God stood by and did nothing." But neither did God reduce Cain to a puppet. In this powerful story, God's intervention was not an intrusion or a negation of Cain's moral agency. Instead, God is portrayed as gently but persistently probing Cain with a series of questions: "Why are you angry, and why has your countenance fallen? If you do well, will you not be accepted? And if you do not do well, sin is lurking at the door; its desire is for you, but you must master it" (vv. 6-7).

God did not overrule Cain's seething hatred. God simply spoke to Cain, asked him questions, and invited him to exercise his agency in a more positive, loving way. But God would not coerce Cain—and therefore, God allowed human bloodshed to break loose.

Original Sin and Prevenient Grace

In the violence committed by brother against brother, we encounter a profound portrait of what Christian tradition has called original sin. It means refusing to trust in God and instead enthroning ourselves as the center and lord of our world. Cain had his moment during which God appealed to him not to surrender to the hateful impulse, but instead to "do well" (v. 7) and avoid the sin crouching at the door.

Could Cain have chosen otherwise than he did? Christian tradition affirms that Cain could indeed have responded positively to God's wooing. If he could not have resisted the temptation toward violence, he cannot be held responsible for his deed. On the other hand, our faith recognizes that once sin had become a reality in the world, a negative momentum was underway. Cain was still responsible, but his act is more understandable in a world in which rivalries, jealousies, and mistrust are already woven into the fabric of human relations. While this narrative shows that God tried to persuade Cain not to yield to the momentum of sin, in the end, Cain was left to decide.

Accordingly, the great second-century theologian Irenaeus insisted that even though sin tyrannizes us with a kind of violent greed, God refuses to redeem creation "by force." God instead redeems us "by persuasion, as it is fitting for God to receive what he wishes by gentleness and not by force." Presumably this is "fitting for God" because it is in keeping with God's nature as self-emptying, other-receiving love. Irenaeus continues: "So neither was the standard of what is just infringed nor did the ancient creation of God perish." This apparently means that God's "ancient creation" includes human agency and responsibility, and it would not be just, or in accordance with God's purposes in creation, simply to change the rules and force compliance upon the world. Such an act of God, indeed, would have spelled the destruction (or "perishing") of God's creation. Obviously, destroying creation is a far cry from redeeming it. Hence, God redeems "by persuasion."[3] Similarly, another

---

3. Cyril C. Richardson, ed, *The Library of Christian Classics*, Vol. I: Early Christian Fathers. (Philadelphia, Westminster Press, 1953), 385, 386. The citation is from Irenaeus' Against Heresies.

second-century Christian writer insisted that God "willed to save man by persuasion, not by compulsion, for compulsion is not God's way of working."[4]

John Wesley was sympathetic to this stream of early Christian thought. But he also understood the power of original sin in human lives to be so strong that only God's own Holy Spirit laboring in our lives (prevenient grace) could enable us to resist the weighty momentum of sin's power. Yet even here, Wesley insisted, God does not work irresistibly so as to force us into faith and obedience. Similarly, in Genesis 4, God did not violate Cain's freedom. In Rabbi Peli's reflections upon Cain's abuse of freedom, I recall that he asked, "Where was God when one-fourth of the human population was destroyed in one blow?" Only one answer is possible: God was right there with Cain every moment, trying to persuade him to choose life over death.

Much of Scripture and tradition affirm, in fact, that God has been "right there" in every moment of all persons' lives everywhere, trying to draw us all toward divine love, mercy and life. But we have made it difficult for ourselves to hear God's voice or to be receptive to the Holy Spirit, precisely by the accumulated tendency to suppress those whispers of grace just as Cain did. Our suppression of God's call, as it has snowballed down through the centuries and crept into our collective consciousness, is original sin. The fact that we all are affected by this original sin is a sign of human solidarity as well as of human idolatry. Whether we like it or not, our lives are intertwined in such a way that the sin of one destructively affects the lives of all, like the ripples of a pebble thrown into a pond.

But if God created us for a life of self-giving and other-receiving love, then sin is not an essential aspect of human nature, despite its power in human life and history. Sin is an intruder. Sin is not to be identified with natural human

---

4. Ibid., 219. The quotation is from the document called The Letter to Diognetus.

limitations, finitude, or shortcomings; rather, it is the fundamental act of rebellion against the God who is Love. If we have been created for fellowship with God and with one another, then to make ourselves strangers to this great Love is to "miss the mark," the New Testament's primary metaphor for sin. It is to "fall short of the glory of God" (Rom. 3:23)—to fall short of God's likeness and image in our lives, to miss the mark of God's ideal calling for us in Christ Jesus.

The Debate between Augustine and Pelagius

Our recognition of human solidarity in this chapter pushes us another step. None of us makes this kind of decision in isolation. The Bible does not teach that we are each our own Adam or Eve. Essentially, it was this point that marked the famous fifth-century debate between Augustine and Pelagius. Emphasizing the biblical idea of human solidarity, Augustine argued that Adam's sin has resulted in humanity's universal bondage to sin. In Augustine's interpretation, human beings are utterly enslaved to sin's power, and only divine grace can save us. Augustine veered toward predestination as a result, claiming that certain human beings are divinely favored and chosen by God, since it cannot have been humanity's choice to believe and repent.

Pelagius, on the other hand, feared that people influenced by such teaching would tend to dismiss responsibility for their own actions; they could conveniently blame Adam. Pelagius countered by insisting that Adam's sin does not negatively affect human freedom, except in giving us a poor example of how to behave. Pelagius, then, taught that human freedom is not essentially hindered by Adam's sin, and that God's grace is manifested quite naturally in our God-given freedom. Indeed we are our own Adam and Eve, argued Pelagius.

This argument pushed Augustine and Pelagius to extremes. Augustine's ideas on original sin and predestination tended to turn humans into little more than pawns. Pelagius's ideas on unmitigated human freedom tended to make human beings into isolated units of individual freedom. We do not have to take Augustine's extreme position in order to recognize that Pelagius did not do justice to the reality of our solidarity; he did not see that what each of us says, does, and thinks profoundly impacts and influences those around us, and vice versa. Furthermore, Pelagius did not recognize that no one comes into this world with a clean slate, precisely because the world into which we come is already blighted by sin. We are members of one another, and thus the sin of our ancestors continues profoundly to affect, and indeed infect, us all.

Augustine's interpretations of original sin and divine predestination led to an extreme understanding of God that would later reappear in the Protestant Reformation: God decrees certain individuals for salvation, and since human beings are enslaved to sin, they can have no real choice in the matter. For Augustine, and for Luther and Calvin over a thousand years later, God is merciful even to save anybody at all, since all of humanity is a "damned mass."

Yet the Bible holds us accountable, so that no matter what we might say about the reality of original sin that surrounds and infests us even before our birth, it cannot lessen our sense of responsibility before God. This tension between solidarity/sin and individuality/responsibility would eventually be resolved, at least for Wesleyan Christians, by an appeal to the doctrine of prevenient grace. As we found in the story of Cain, the idea of prevenient grace is that God is ever-present in our lives, enabling us, if we will, to desire and even choose the divine will. God's Spirit and Word can be resisted, but if we yield to Him, we can experience true freedom by loving and serving God and our neighbor. While in one sense a fuller explication of the doctrine of prevenient grace must await a later chapter in the Story of God, in another, profoundly biblical sense, it is the very basis for what is sooner to follow in Chapter 4: a theology of divine-human *covenants*.

Reflect on this...

What are your thoughts and feelings after reading this chapter?

How has this chapter helped you better understand the Story of God?

In what ways are you involved in this part of God's Story today?

The People of Israel in God's Story:

The Doctrine of Covenants

The story the Bible tells begins with God's goodness in creating this world, then moves to humanity's rebellion and God's persistent goodness in seeking our redemption. These themes surface early; already in the story of Eden we faced with the One who patiently and lovingly haunts us. This God of redemption seeks sinners with probing questions like "Where are you?" and "Where is your brother?"

Such questions might seem laughable, coming from an omnipotent, omnipresent and omniscient God—but perhaps that is just the point. The "omni" doctrines pay all kinds of metaphysical compliments to God, but seem to overlook the central biblical affirmation that God is a God of relation. The God of this Story calls into being a world that is truly distinct from its Creator; the world is neither an extension of God's being nor an elaborate puppet show. God has granted us the gift of otherness. Thus, we humans are creatures who can both seek God and flee God, who can cooperate with God or rebel against God, who can reflect upon God or categorically deny God. We humans are creatures who exercise the power of conscious choice, which is perhaps the greatest evidence of our otherness from God.

Scripture is clear in insisting that this situation is precisely what God wills. We are actually made by God with the capacity to say no to God. This is apparently necessary for true and honest relationship. I cannot be in true relationship with that which is not other than who and what I am; to borrow from the great Jewish philosopher Martin Buber (1878-1965), in the true I-Thou encounter, the Thou must truly be Thou to me: "I become through my relation to the Thou; as I become I, I say Thou. All real living is meeting."[5] Buber is not speaking only (or even primarily) of relationship to God, but of the possibility of

5. Martin Buber, *I and Thou*, trans. Ronald Gregor Smith (New York: Charles Scriber's Sons, 1958), 11.

relationship at all; it is only in our otherness from God, from other people, and from the world that we can give or receive the grace of relation.

So also it is with our Maker: God does not control us, but calls us. God does not manipulate us, but beckons to us. Before God is anything else, God is Love—the Love who creates us, sustains us, and longingly seeks us out, all for the sake of give-and-receive relations.

We encounter notions like these dramatically, and powerfully, in the Bible's stories of the covenants (Latin, *co* = together; *vene* = come) that God initiates. This idea that God is the God of covenants, of pacts or agreements, is too often ignored in theology, to its own detriment. To say that God is a covenantal God is to suggest a divine interest in our cooperation, a divine commitment to partnership, and a divine power that empowers and affirms us poor creatures of dust.

In Chapter 2 we dealt with God as Creator and the world as God's creation. In Chapter 3 we saw this risky process of creation unfold with the painful reality of human rebellion. In this chapter, we shall attempt to tell the Story of divine grace—of God's stubborn, persistent desire to love and redeem this fallen creation—as revealed especially in the covenant he initiated with Israel through Moses. There are other covenants described in the Bible, of course,[6] but it is indisputable that the gift of Torah (the Law) resides at the heart of God's dealings with Israel.

All covenants described in Scripture are established by divine initiative, reminding us that they are all grounded in grace and not in human imagination or ability. The Wesleyan tradition has tended to call this grace

---

6. *Renewal in Love*, chapter 3.

prevenient (Latin, *pre* = prior to; *vene* = come) to emphasize that it is always God who makes the first move toward us in covenantal relationship.

All of the biblical covenants originate and are sustained in God's gracious love for creation. But the fact that these are covenants also reminds us that God chooses not to redeem us apart from our willing cooperation. For this reason, Wesley delighted to quote a little line from Augustine: "He who made us without ourselves will not save us without ourselves." That is, the God who created us without asking our permission will not redeem us without our cooperation. Just as surely as covenants are grounded in God's prevenient grace, so also this grace evokes, encourages, and empowers us to be co-operators with God (cf. 2 Cor. 5:18). One of the great mysteries of the Bible is that God Almighty bends low into creation to covenant with human beings, to work together with them toward God's vision of *shalom* for the world.

God's Gracious Gift of the Torah

We have already noted that the Exodus of the people Israel from Egyptian bondage is the central revelatory event in Jewish history. This deliverance cast its light even upon Jewish creation theology: God called forth a people of covenantal dignity out of the chaotic darkness of slavery, delivering them by separating the threatening waters of the sea.

But this fundamental, formative event was not an end in itself. Just as God called creation into being for the sake of true relations of love, so God delivered this multitude of Jewish slaves for the sake of their relationship to God as the people of God. They were not simply liberated, for the flip side of the Exodus event is the covenant initiated on Mount Sinai. The brief prelude to the Ten Commandments reveals the inseparability of the Exodus and Sinai: "I am the Lord your God, who brought you out of the land of Egypt, out of the house of slavery; you shall have no other gods before me" (Exod. 20:2-3).

Simply put, the "law" of Sinai arises out of the "grace" of Exodus. The important implication for the Story of God is that grace is joined with obligation, gift with task, and freedom with responsibility. The German theologian Dietrich Bonhoeffer said it well: there is no "cheap grace."

There is, however, an old tendency within Christian teaching to understand the Sinai covenant not as grace at all, but only as harsh, unbending law meant to frustrate people into a sense of their own sinfulness and inability. It is difficult, however, to support such an interpretation on the basis of the biblical text. The Hebrew term *torah* is better translated as "way" than as "law." For centuries of Judaism, the Torah has not been seen or experienced as an excessive burden; it is, rather, God's gift to Israel as a way to live as God's people in the world. The divine revelation to Moses was not of a harsh taskmaster, but of "the Lord, a God merciful and gracious, slow to anger, and abounding in steadfast love and faithfulness, keeping steadfast love for the thousandth generation, forgiving iniquity and transgression and sin" (34:6-7), who is just in punishing the guilty.

The essential portrait of the God of Israel, then, is a God of love and mercy, whose Torah is a gift that leads to life: "See, I have set before you today life and prosperity, death and adversity . . . Choose life so that you and your descendants may live, loving the Lord your God, obeying him, and holding fast to him" (Deut. 30:15, 19-20).

Divine Grace Implies Human Obligation

Perhaps we have sufficiently established the utter graciousness that undergirds God's gift of the Torah to the people Israel. It is crucial to remember that this grace also includes obligation. God, according to the Story, chose this people called Israel to be "a priestly kingdom," mediators between God and creation. This people, visibly marked obedience to the Torah, was to be "a holy nation," set apart from all other peoples in order to be God's "treasured possession" (Exod. 19:5-6). In other words, in his covenant with this particular people, Israel, God renewed the initial intent of creation—that all human beings should represent God, in whose image they were created. The covenant, then, was offered to this particular people for the sake of blessing all creation and with the redemption of all peoples in mind; God commandeered the people of Israel precisely because "the whole earth is [his]" (v. 5). This has often been called the scandal of particularity: that the God of the entire created order, the universal Creator and Sustainer, works in very specific, particular, and historical ways to redeem fallen humanity.

It is for this divine work of redemption, then, that the people Israel were graciously called into covenant at Sinai. In obedience to the conditions of the covenant, Israel was to embody God's love and concern for every detail of human existence. God called the people to share in divine holiness and love, and to embody this holiness and love in their life together.

This helps to explain the intent of the second commandment of the Decalogue, which prohibits fashioning "an idol, whether in the form of anything that is in heaven above, or that is on the earth beneath, or that is in the water under the earth" (20:4). One reason for this, to be sure, was to guard Israel from the polytheism of their neighbors, who tended toward all sorts of idolatrous practices. Another was to teach them that divine majesty cannot be captured in figures of wood and stone. But another, often overlooked reason for this command was that, because God cannot be physically represented, the Holy One could be encountered only in a commanding Voice and represented in human obedience. The Creator of all things is not to be visualized or objectified, but to be heard and obeyed. All of this is well-stated in Deuteronomy 4:

[Remember] how you once stood before the Lord your God at Horeb [Sinai] . . . [Y]ou approached and stood at the foot of the mountain while the mountain was blazing up to the very heavens, shrouded in dark clouds. Then the Lord spoke to you out of the fire. You heard the sound of words but saw no form; there was only a voice. He declared to you his covenant, which he charged you to observe, that is, the ten commandments; and he wrote them on two stone tablets. . . . Since you saw no form when the Lord spoke to you at Horeb out of the fire, take care and watch yourselves closely, so that you do not act corruptly by making an idol for yourselves, in the form of any figure . . . But the Lord has taken you and brought you out of the iron-smelter, out of Egypt, to become a people of his very own possession, as you are now. (vv. 10-13, 15-16, 20)

The people Israel were denied physical images of God precisely so that, in their obedience to the Sinai covenant, they themselves would represent the image of God—the image in which all people are created and to which God desires to restore all people, beginning with the people Israel. This notion is powerfully presented in another Deuteronomy passage:

For the Lord your God is God of gods and Lord of lords, the great God, mighty and awesome, who is not partial and takes no bribe; who executes justice for the orphan and the widow, and who loves the strangers, providing them food and clothing. You shall also love the stranger, for you were strangers in the land of Egypt. (10:17-19)

The Exodus passage above reminds us that the Holy One is not content that Israel (or we) simply offer up our praises, lauding God as Creator and Sustainer of all things. True worship inevitably involves hearing God's call and responding by investing ourselves in God's redeeming activity. It is easy to become fixated on a mental image of God as in Deuteronomy 10:17, lifted from its context—God, the almighty Ruler of the universe, the great, the mighty, the awesome God who is always just. But mental images of God can be just as idolatrous as metal images of God if they do not move us to a life lived in imitation of the One who created us. This is the obligation of the Sinai covenant, grounded in grace, which God initiated with Israel through Moses.

Grace and obligation, gift and task—these are inseparably linked in the logic of Sinai. Further, it is clear that this grace is bestowed on Israel for the sake of all the nations, all peoples everywhere. In this covenant at Sinai, God graciously elects a people who will function as divine representatives, who will be a kingdom of priests to the other nations, because all of creation is God's, and he intends to redeem and restore all of creation. ●

Reflect on this...

What are your thoughts and feelings after reading this chapter?

How has this chapter helped you better understand the Story of God?

In what ways are you involved in this part of God's Story today?

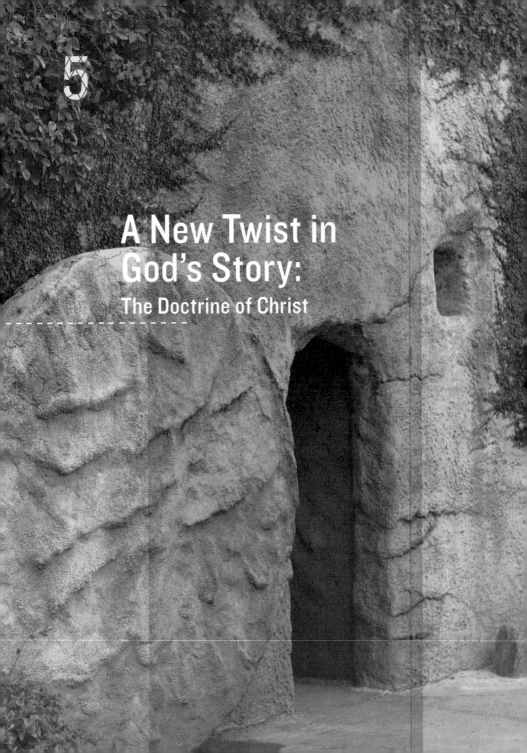

5

A New Twist in God's Story:

The Doctrine of Christ

As we follow the plot of the Story of God as found in Scripture, we now reach a decisive turn, a new twist in the telling. We have heard of the loving Creator who, out of everlasting love and in the interests of faithful covenantal relation, calls the entire universe into being. We have witnessed the tragic rebellion of the creature most specifically created for faithful covenant, the human. We have read that the Creator, in persistent love, has initiated the gracious process of restoring humanity, and all of creation, to faithful partnership through the establishment of covenants. But now the Christian telling of this Story begins to diverge from the Jewish. For now, in the person of Jesus of Nazareth, Christians confess that a new and decisive covenant has been established.

But even as we begin to talk about a divergence from the Jewish telling of God's Story and about a new covenant through Jesus, we ought not to overstate Christianity's difference or distance from Judaism. Christians on the whole could profit by deeper appreciation for what the Jews and their history have meant for Christianity. Apart from the faithfulness of Jews to God and Torah through the centuries before Jesus, there would be no Story for us to tell. Paul warned early Gentile Christians against a superior attitude toward Jews who had not responded positively to the gospel (Rom. 11:17-18, 24).

A Covenantal Context for Christ

All of this means that we ought to recognize the importance of the history of the people Israel to correctly understand the mission of Jesus. Biblical faith is rooted in history, and particularly the history of the Jewish people as the elect people of God. It bears repeating that Jesus himself was a Jew! In order to understand his life and ministry well, we need to situate Jesus within the history, culture, and religious traditions of his people.

Thus, Christian leaders showed good judgment in the second century when they condemned the ideas of a popular teacher named Marcion as heresy. Marcion believed that Christians should have nothing to do with the Hebrew Scriptures (what we now call the Old Testament). In putting together his own scriptural canon, Marcion kept only Paul's letters and the gospel of Luke, but did a scissors-and-paste job on those documents to make them sound as un-Jewish as possible. When he proposed that Christians should cut themselves off from their historical and religious roots in the Jewish people's covenantal life before God, Church leaders replied that the God of Israel is none other than the God and Father of our Lord Jesus Christ.

When the early Christian leaders rejected Marcion, they demonstrated faithfulness to the New Testament writings, which assume the importance of Israel's history with God as the proper context for understanding the significance of Jesus Christ. The creation of the universe, the making of humanity in God's image, the human fall into sin, the calling of Israel into covenant, the priests, prophets, and kings anointed by God—the whole of God's Story—was now recited in a new light, "the light of the knowledge of the glory of God in the face of Jesus Christ" (2 Cor. 4:6). Yet it was also told in the strong conviction that the coming of Jesus was a faithful continuation of God's labor in the history of the people of Israel; in Paul's words, "Christ has become a servant of the circumcised on behalf of the truth of God in order that he might confirm the promises given to the patriarchs" (Rom. 15:8).

The critical point for our consideration, then, is that the Story we have heard so far—a Story of divine love expressed in God's "Let there be" toward creation, of divine humility expressed in the willingness to work in covenant partnership—now moves to a new and glorious depth of love and humility in Jesus Christ. But what God does in Christ is not essentially unlike what

God was already doing in creation and in covenant—emptying himself in outpouring love, calling forth a people in and for covenantal faithfulness. For when God entered into this world through Christ, he came not in infinite splendor that would overwhelm or negate human identity or agency; in fact, our Creator did precisely the opposite by coming to us as a human servant, a covenant partner, a faithful Son who constantly prayed to the Father, "Not what I want, but what you want" (Mark 14:36; cf. John 8:29). In other words, just as we have already seen that God's power is primarily an empowering love of the creature and that God's activity enlists and enables partnership, so now, in the person of Jesus, we see God's power and activity most clearly revealed in the freely offered obedience of this faithful Son, this covenant Partner (Rom. 5:17-19).

One Crucial New Testament Portrait of Jesus

These considerations provide the necessary covenantal context for Christ so that we can understand Jesus in terms of God's gracious, saving activity in the history of the Jewish people. Matthew is the Gospel writer most obviously committed to interpreting Jesus in this way. Matthew's underlying theme is the deep significance of Israel's history for appreciating the identity and ministry of Jesus.

Israel's history with God is so important to Matthew, in fact, that he begins with it when he tells Jesus' story. In introducing the Messiah's genealogy, Matthew identifies Jesus as "the son of David, the son of Abraham" (1:1). To be David's son was to be an heir in David's royal line, and for the Jewish people, King David represented the height of Israel's glory. When they dreamed of a messiah, they often had someone like David in mind—someone who would restore that glory. Matthew's genealogy proclaims Jesus as Israel's new David, the fulfillment of God's history with Israel.

In order to demonstrate this, Matthew begins the genealogy with Abraham, the father of the people Israel, and moves down through the generations to Jesus, "who is called the Messiah" (v. 16). Conversely, the other Gospel with a genealogy, Luke, begins with Jesus and traces backward all the way to Adam. (Luke apparently is more concerned with demonstrating that Jesus is the Second Adam, the new and ultimate human being.)

But we must also give attention to the latter part of Matthew's description of Jesus: "son of Abraham" (v. 1). Abraham was not only the beginning point of what would become the people of Israel but also the one who believed God's promise that, through his descendants, all the peoples of the earth would be blessed (Gen. 12:2-3). Thus, Abraham is important to all peoples, Jews and Gentiles, as Paul argues in Romans 4 and Galatians 3. This is a theological point driven home in the genealogy itself; in tracing Jesus' lineage, Matthew does the unusual by including women—and not good Jewish women, or even just any women, but women like the following:

- Tamar (Matt. 1:3), whose sordid story is told in Genesis 38;
- Rahab (v. 5), a Canaanite prostitute who sheltered Joshua's spies in Jericho;
- Ruth (v. 5), a Moabite, who cunningly arranged her own marriage to Boaz; and
- Bathsheba (v. 6), who committed adultery with King David.

It was odd enough, in that patriarchal culture, to mention women in a genealogy. But if Matthew was going to include women in his genealogy of Jesus, why these? In each case, they can be fairly described as at least mildly scandalous—yet through them God labored to bring forth the Messiah! Matthew is proclaiming the mysterious and unpredictable grace of God.

And so we see Jesus: Son of David, King of Israel, God's holy anointed One; but also Son of Abraham, a descendant of some rough-living Gentiles with skeletons in the closet. Truly his genealogy is a proclamation of "Emmanuel," God with us (Matt. 1:23).

God's Calling upon Israel

This grace has come to fruition through God's involvement with the people of Israel: Jesus embodies the story of Israel in his own story. In him we see fully who and what God is, and what it looks like to be a faithful child of the covenant. Indeed, in passages that are unique to Matthew's Gospel, Jesus is presented as having understood his earthly ministry to be directed toward gathering and renewing the people of Israel (10:5-6; 15:21-28). But if the ultimate intention of God's covenant with Israel was to make them a nation of priests for the sake of all peoples, then Jesus' embodiment of Israel's story could not help but finally extend beyond Israel's borders. This, in fact, is what we discover in the Great Commission, which involves making disciples "of all nations" (28:19).

But first things first: let us appreciate a few of the ways in which Matthew's account roots Jesus firmly in Israel's soil. Matthew is the only Gospel that tells us of Herod's attempt to be rid of the "King of the Jews" by killing Jewish boys in the Bethlehem area (2:2, 16-18); the Pharaoh's attempt to solve Egypt's "Jewish problem" by drowning Hebrew boys back in the book of Exodus looms in the textual background. Matthew is the only Gospel that tells of Joseph and Mary taking the child with them to Egypt to elude Herod, and thus the only one who tells of their "exodus" from Egypt (2:15) back to the land of promise. But unlike the first son, Israel, whom God called out of Egypt only to have to deal with his collective disobedience (Hos. 11:1-3), this Son, Jesus, lives a life of faithful covenant obedience.

There is no better evidence of Jesus' faithfulness to the God of the covenants than his forty-day period of fasting, praying, and facing temptation in the wilderness, all of which parallels Israel's forty years of wandering in the wilderness. In these wilderness temptations, Jesus embodied and relived the history of his ancestral people; as they were led by the cloud of God's presence to the testing grounds of their wilderness wanderings, so "Jesus was led up by the Spirit into the wilderness to be tempted by the devil" (Matt. 4:1).

The first temptation (Matt. 4:2-4) concerned turning stones into bread. Jesus' own hunger pangs raised the issue of whether the messianic mission would involve social reform and gaining followers by feeding their stomachs. Of course, there is nothing wrong with feeding people; it is simply that physical sustenance by itself is insufficient—for "One does not live by bread alone, but by every word that comes from the mouth of God" (v. 4). But there is more going on here: Israel's history in the wilderness. When Jesus quoted Moses's statement about living not only on bread but on the divine Word (Deut. 8:3), he was citing words that were "not, in their own context, addressed to an individual but to a whole covenant-people. . . . If Israel had been allowed to hunger, to be humbled, and to be fed with no ordinary food [but rather with manna], then ought not he who was repeating that experience also endure the same trials?"[7]

Jesus' second temptation (Matt. 4:5-7) was to achieve recognition and a following through sensationalism, through marvelous wonders that would catapult him to popularity. Jesus again quoted the words of Moses: "Do not put the Lord your God to the test" (v. 7), which in their original context (Deut. 6:16) referred to Israel's doubt of God's presence with them at Massah (Exod. 17:6-7). The appeal to sensationalism does "put God to the test"

---

7. W. F. Albright and C. S. Mann, *Matthew,* in the Anchor Bible. (Garden City, N.Y.: Doubleday and Co., 1971), 36.

because it is rooted in unbelief about God's covenantal faithfulness. Even in the wilderness, Jesus refused to put God to that test.

Finally, Jesus was tempted to compromise with evil in order to gain political and material power (Matt. 4:8-10). He once again responded to temptation with words that Moses had spoken to Israel: "Worship the Lord your God, and serve only him" (v. 10; cf. Deut. 6:13). In responding to this third temptation, Jesus refused to do some secular calculation about how he might bring about better results in his ministry. In trusting in the goodness of the Father's will, he refused to compromise, trusting that in the proper time God would give him "all authority in heaven and on earth" (Matt. 28:18).

For Matthew, Jesus was a new Moses, delivered from the Pharaoh's hand and brought forth out of Egypt; but Jesus was also the covenant Son of Israel, choosing to rely on the words of Moses and live faithfully by those words. Unlike the Israelites who wandered for 40 years and so often rejected the divine Word spoken through Moses, Jesus relied on that Word, and in the empowering presence of the Spirit, lived the life of God's faithful, obedient Son.

Reflect on this...

What are your thoughts and feelings after reading this chapter?

How has this chapter helped you better understand the Story of God?

In what ways are you involved in this part of God's Story today?

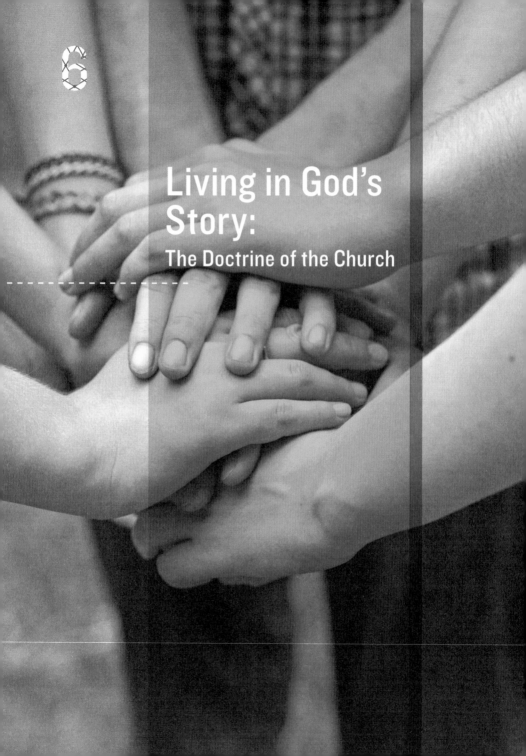

6

Living in God's Story:
The Doctrine of the Church

When we turn to the doctrine of the Church, we are seeking to understand our present location in the Story of God. For it is within the context and historical traditions of the Church that we find ourselves in this moment, seeking to trace the flow, direction, and meaning of God's Story. The Church is a body of believers that has been gathered together by God through Christ in the power of the Spirit to testify to the Story of salvation, and to worship the One around whom the Story revolves.

The Church transcends the normal human boundaries of generation and geography. It includes people of widely divergent denominations, languages, cultures, colors, and historical eras. This variety makes for an incredible richness and diversity of expression in the Church's worship of the living God. The rallying point of the Church is not a common worship style or cultural expression, but the Triune God who acts decisively for redemption of all creation.

A Gospel Story

The Gospels are bursting with stories that put vibrance and color into the doctrine of God's saving work through Jesus Christ! Even so, there is one story recorded in all three Synoptic Gospels that is particularly revealing of the saving power of Jesus in the face of the forces that distort and corrupt human life. It is the "horror story" of Jesus' encounter with the demoniac in the graveyard.

What is so striking about this story is that it demonstrates how far Jesus was, and is, willing to go to redeem and restore human lives. It reminds us that the Church is the community of the redeemed who are being restored through Christ to the life God always intended for humanity: life in the image of God (Col. 3:10-17). In order to fully appreciate this, let us consider what this gospel story proclaims:

- First, Jesus and the twelve disciples had sailed across the Sea of Galilee and disembarked in "the country of the Gerasenes" (Mark 5:1), a predominantly Gentile region. Any first-century Jewish reader of the Gospel would have already begun to feel uneasy about where this story was going.

- Next, we read that "a man out of the tombs" confronted Jesus and his disciples (v. 2). According to Jewish law, touching a corpse rendered a person ritually unclean for a week (Num. 19:11). On top of being a Gentile, this desperate man bore the disgrace of living among the dead, exiled from human community.

- Luke added that the man "had worn no clothes . . . for a long time" (8:27)—more shame. Mark added that the man gashed his naked body with graveyard stones (5:5), another unclean act according to Jewish law (Lev. 19:28).

- As one level of uncleanness piled up on another, Mark also reports that the man was possessed by "an unclean spirit" (5:2). The "uncleanness" of the story was reaching hellish proportions.

- As if all this were not enough, we read later that this naked, bruised and bleeding Gentile with an unclean spirit, wandering among the tombs, lived near a herd of pigs—unclean animals, according to Jewish law.

For any self-respecting Jew, the entire situation reeked of what would have been an unbearable stench of utterly unapproachable impurity. This truly was a horror story of epic proportions! Yet into this desperately frightful situation Jesus strode as the living Lord of love, offering redemption to this ruined, seemingly hopeless life. Jesus is the salvation of God amid fallen creation! Rather than treat the man like the rest of his village had by depriving him of identity and dehumanizing him with exile and chains, Jesus confronted this nameless victim as a person of worth, asking his name (Mark 5:9). And after

Jesus exorcised the unclean spirits ("Legion") that tormented him, those who knew the man saw him "sitting there, clothed and in his right mind . . . and they were afraid" (v. 15). This was a new and very different horror story! The mighty deliverance Jesus brought to this miserable outcast so unsettled the people of the nearby city that they begged Jesus to leave (v. 17).

What we see in this story is that there is no situation, no matter how bleak or apparently hopeless, into which Jesus is unwilling or unable to bring divine healing and deliverance. We should ask whether there are such "horror stories" which the Church, which is called to be Jesus' community, avoids like the plague today. We need not ask, *What would Jesus do?* We know what Jesus did—he encountered this lonely, frightened, demon-haunted Gentile—an outsider if ever there was one—and restored him to physical, spiritual, and social well-being (vv. 15, 19). Why would we, Christ's Church, ever presume that anyone is beyond hope?

Salvation Offered to All

The same compassionate mercy and power of God that led Jesus through a Gentile graveyard would later lead him to a Roman cross to pour out his life and blood for all. And in the Wesleyan tradition of Christian faith, we really do mean *all*. According to the Scriptures, God does not desire "any to perish, but all to come to repentance" (2 Pet. 3:9). But the fact is that many do not come to repentance—this is a most sobering piece of evidence that not everything God wills actually comes to fruition. But still, Wesleyan tradition insists that God desires all people to be redeemed and restored through Jesus. Christ lived, died, and now lives for all. And while the grace of God does not overwhelm the human will, God is persistent. This is embodied by Jesus' refusal to leave the man in his demonic oppression, despite his pleas that Jesus not "torment" him (Mark 5:7).

This man's bondage reminds us that we do not and cannot save ourselves. God, in his unfathomable mercy, saves us. There is a real sense in which we, enslaved to sin and spiritually dead (Eph. 2:1-3; Rom. 6:17-21), are every bit as helpless as the Garasene demoniac. It is only as Jesus the Savior strides mightily and mercifully into our impoverished condition that we may taste redemption. Titus 3:3-7 states this truth with clarity and power:

> "For we ourselves were once foolish, disobedient, led astray, slaves to various passions and pleasures, passing our days in malice and envy, despicable, hating one another. But when the goodness and loving kindness of God our Savior appeared, he saved us, not because of any works of righteousness that we had done, but according to his mercy, through the water of rebirth and renewal by the Holy Spirit. This Spirit he poured out on us richly through Jesus Christ our Savior, so that, having been justified by his grace, we might become heirs according to the hope of eternal life."

This passage reflects three different aspects of God's salvation in Christ as it mightily impacts our lives: justification, regeneration, and adoption. Let us briefly give attention to each of these.

The aspect of conversion known as justification is clearly reflected in the words, "God our Savior . . . saved us, not because of any works of righteousness that we had done, but according to his mercy . . . having been justified by his grace." The apostle Paul calls Jesus the One in whom all of God's promises find their amen, their validation (2 Cor. 1:20). This means we can look to the life and words of Jesus to discover the nature of God's promises to us. In the Story of Jesus, we hear that God already loves us, already offers us forgiveness, and has already reconciled the world to himself. All we are asked to do is receive those promises and live in their light. This is the justification by grace through faith that was at the heart of Martin

Luther's Reformation proclamation: there is nothing we can do to earn or add to the offer of grace that God makes to us in Jesus Christ.

Regeneration, the second aspect of Christian conversion, is reflected in the words of the Titus passage: "through the water of rebirth and renewal by the Holy Spirit . . . poured out on us richly through Jesus Christ our Savior." To regenerate literally means "to bring to life again," or "to bring new life to," which is precisely what God's Holy Spirit, the Life-Giver, does in conversion and Christian baptism. We are, in the maternal imagery Jesus used in his conversation with Nicodemus, given rebirth or "born from above" by the Spirit (John 3:3, 7). Paul describes the same reality of transformation begun in our lives by writing that "God's love has been poured into our hearts through the Holy Spirit that has been given to us" (Rom. 5:5).

Since the Spirit pours God into our hearts is the Spirit who was decisively revealed in the person of Jesus, the transformation that begins is one that steers our hearts and lives toward Christlikeness. We know that we are not entirely transformed in the moment of conversion so that there is no need for further transformation and growth; conversion is simply the beginning of the process whereby we are being "conformed to the image of his Son" (Rom. 8:29). It is a process that will not be completed until we see Jesus (1 John 3:2). This lifelong process of becoming increasingly Christlike in thought, word, and deed is part of what we mean by sanctification. In conversion, we already are embarking on the path of being made holy. That is why Paul, in his letter to the Christians in Rome, could call them to "present your bodies as a living sacrifice, holy and acceptable to God, which is spiritual worship" (Rom. 12:1) with full confidence that this "offering of the Gentiles" could be "acceptable, sanctified by the Holy Spirit" (Rom. 15:16).

A third dimension of Christian conversion, adoption, is reflected in the words of the letter to Titus: "that . . . we might become heirs according to the hope of eternal life" (3:7). To be an heir is to be a rightful inheritor, a member of the family. Paul states that "all who are being led by the Spirit of God are children of God," and that we "have received a spirit of adoption" (Rom. 8:14, 15). Being adopted into the family of God at the moment of conversion gives us the freedom to approach God with boldness and honesty and to cry out in the Spirit of Jesus as he cried out in the garden of Gethsemane: "Abba! Father!" (v. 15; Gal. 4:6; cf. Mark 14:36). Of course, becoming a child of the Father also means we enter into a family with many brothers and sisters—the local church, which is the body of Christ (1 Cor. 12:27).

Thus, the imagery of adoption inevitably reminds us that Christian conversion is always conversion into a community of faith. We are baptized into a Christian family that precedes us and surrounds us with love and encouragement, that celebrates the great Story of God's redemption each day. God's Spirit, who witnesses to our adoption by crying "Abba!" within our hearts (Rom. 8:15; Gal. 4:6) is the same Spirit in whom all believers share (1 Cor. 12:7, 13). The reality of *koinōnia,* or mutual sharing in God's outpoured Spirit, should press us to realize our need for one another; we are placed in the body of Christ to encourage and help each other to tell and live the Story of God.

Back to the Gospel Story

The "horror story" of Gerasene demoniac provides us with a portrait of the many-faceted miracle of Christian conversion:

- Jesus' willingness to march into the death and decay of the tombs to meet the possessed and oppressed man, and there to ask his name, is a portrait of God's unconditional love that welcomes us as we are— *justification.*

- Jesus' transformation of this ravaged, anguished man into a confident and calm person, "clothed and in his right mind" (Mark 5:15), is a portrait of the radical change in heart and character we are offered in *regeneration*.
- Jesus' restoration of the man to the family and society that had exiled him, so that he might re-enter human relationships of mutual care and love rather than continue in the horror and loneliness of the tombs, is a portrayal of *adoption*.

There is a final point: This man, redeemed from the destructive powers of hell, "began to proclaim . . . how much Jesus had done for him" (5:20). That is *evangelism*. May we, the disciples Jesus calls his Church, go and do likewise!

Reflect on this...

What are your thoughts and feelings after reading this chapter?

How has this chapter helped you better understand the Story of God?

In what ways are you involved in this part of God's Story today?

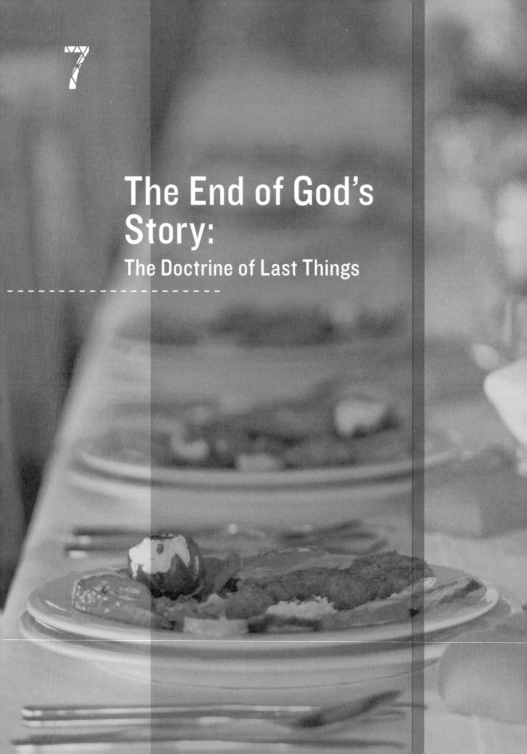

7

The End of God's Story:

The Doctrine of Last Things

The doctrine of eschatology (Greek, *eschaton* = last or end) has to do with the hope in Christ associated with the end of God's Story. For what are we hoping? How do we expect that it will all come out, and why?

When eschatology becomes the focus, it is not unusual for speculation and argument to thrive. The doctrine of eschatology will always generate plenty of controversy and excitement because it has to do with expectations and anxieties about an unknown future.

The Coming One and His Coming Kingdom

For this reason, it is important to keep our ideas about eschatology closely tied to Jesus. In that light, let us consider a fascinating Gospel story. It begins this way: "When John heard in prison what the Messiah was doing, he sent word by his disciples and said to him, 'Are you the one who is to come, or are we to wait for another?'" (Matt. 11:2-3).

This may surprise us. The great prophet who announced Jesus to be the Messiah, who baptized Jesus in the Jordan to launch his ministry, was having his doubts. Matthew's careful wording suggests that the doubts were rooted in what he had heard about "what the Messiah was doing." Jesus was not fulfilling John's expectations about how the Messiah should behave.

The confusion John experienced in his prison cell can readily be traced to the fact that he and Jesus had once seemed to be on the same page, preaching the same message. Indeed, the Gospel of Matthew represents both their messages with identical words: "Repent, for the kingdom of heaven has come near" (3:2; 4:17).

Since this was the message proclaimed by both Jesus and John, it is crucial for us to understand what that message might have meant to those who heard it. When first-century Jews heard that God's kingdom was near, what images or hopes did those words evoke? What had John meant by "the kingdom of heaven"? What did it mean to the disciples when Jesus instructed them to pray for the coming of God's kingdom?

Israel and the Kingdom of God

The phrase "kingdom of God," which is predominant in the Synoptic Gospels, rarely, if ever, appears in the Hebrew scriptures. Nonetheless, the concept of God's kingdom or reign is strongly present. Israel was called out from among the many peoples of the world to be a nation of representatives for God—a kingdom of priests ruled by God (Ex. 19:5-6). God was no less the Ruler of all creation and its peoples when establishing this particular covenantal kingdom; Israel was to represent God to all other peoples because "the whole earth is [God's]."

The concept of God as the King of Israel is also strongly implied in the story of Israel's clamoring for a king. The prophet Samuel insisted that God was to be their King, but God eventually gave in to the Israelites' desire. Saul's royal tenure ended in failure, but he was succeeded by the greatest king in Israel's collective memory: David. When Israel's fortunes faded in subsequent generations, the memory of David's glory remained as a ray of hope: their deliverer would be a righteous king whose glory would surpass even David's. This is why the anticipated Messiah was called "the son of David." It was not primarily a matter of genealogy. Rather, "son of David" meant first of all the one who would come in the spirit of David, under divine anointing, to restore God's rule over Israel and even over all the earth. There is every reason to believe that the people who greeted Jesus during his triumphal entry into Jerusalem believed that he was about to overthrow the pagan occupation and replace it with divine rule: "Hosanna! . . . Blessed is the coming kingdom of our ancestor David!" (Mark 11:9-10).

We know that those eschatological hopes were dashed less than a week later when this anticipated Messiah, rather than having conquered the Romans, was crucified on a Roman cross. There was a big difference between Jewish expectations for the Messiah and what Jesus did. And yet Jesus insisted that the kingdom of God was at hand! If, by the phrase "the kingdom of God," Jesus did not mean what most of his fellow Jews envisioned, what might he have meant instead? I suggest that three aspects of Jesus' ministry shed light on this question.

The Kingdom in Jesus' Parables

First, in Jesus' teachings, and especially in his parables, the kingdom of God is revealed. Recall how often Jesus' parables open with, "The kingdom of heaven is like . . ." Jesus' images for God's kingdom are drawn from a number of everyday experiences: divine rule is like a mustard seed that starts out tiny and eventually grows into a great tree; it is like a woman working a bit of leaven into a lump of dough until the lump is thoroughly leavened; it is like a king who forgives vast debts and expects his subjects to extend such grace to one another; it is like a shepherd who lovingly seeks out the one stray lamb; it is like a woman who rejoices at having discovered a lost coin while cleaning her house. These, of course, are but a sampling of Jesus' kingdom images, but they and many others share an overarching theme: there is much that is unexpected and surprising in God's kingdom. God's delightful unpredictability makes it impossible for human imaginations to fully understand the nature of his coming rule.

God's Kingdom in Jesus' Healings

Second, we see the coming of the Kingdom in Jesus' healings and exorcisms. Jesus was known as One whose teaching, delivered with a sense of authority, was ratified by mighty deeds. His exorcisms were a powerful sign of the approach of God's kingdom, overcoming the powers of darkness and oppression. He proclaimed, "if it is by the Spirit of God that I cast out demons, then the kingdom of God has come to you" (Matt. 12:28).

Similarly, Jesus' ministry of healing, often performed in tandem with his proclamation of God's kingdom (cf. Mark 2:1-12), can be understood as a manifestation of God's future kingdom as it pervaded first-century Galilee in the person of Christ. His acts of healing in the power of the Spirit were incursions from God's future, a foretaste of the "healing of the nations" that God has in store (Rev. 22:2).

God's Kingdom in Jesus' Expansive Love

Third, Jesus expresses and reveals the kingdom of God in his love and humility, particularly as he extends himself to the poor and outcast of his culture. For Jesus, God's kingdom is a kingdom of love—love for neighbor, yes, but more amazingly (and more in line with the nature of divine rule), love for enemy. It was a love that was to encompass the Romans who oppressed them, the Samaritans who despised them, and the tax gatherers who cheated them. While the Pharisees tended to define themselves by the company they kept at the dinner table, Jesus was the honored Guest (and sometimes the Host) of dinner gatherings whose participants could be described as motley at best. Jesus' "table fellowship," as it is often called by contemporary biblical scholars, was undoubtedly a sign of the coming messianic feast in God's kingdom—a feast in which "many will come from east and west [i.e., non-Jews] and will eat with Abraham and Isaac and Jacob in the kingdom of heaven" (Matt. 8:11). Jesus' table fellowship, for which he was roundly criticized by the Pharisees, was a foretaste of this feast in God's coming kingdom.

The Feast of the Coming Kingdom

But Jesus' table fellowship as a sign of God's coming kingdom is most evident in the only miracle reported by all four Gospels: the feeding of the multitudes. In all three Synoptic Gospels, the feeding of the multitudes is immediately preceded by the description of a very different dinner, representing a very different sort of kingdom.

That contrasting dinner is the birthday banquet of Herod. In this feast that parades the politics of power, there were undoubtedly numerous courses of fine foods served by servants. There were dancing girls, political intrigue, inside deals and, after dessert, John the Baptist's head on a platter. Such evil characterizes the kingdoms of this world.

Then came Jesus' kingdom dinner from another world—the world to come. The food was simpler, but everybody had more than enough. Jesus' own disciples were the servants of this meal, distributing blessed bread and fish to men, women, and children. The women were not asked to serve at this meal, let alone dance. And nobody lost his head! Roman banquets, like the one Herod threw to impress his upper-crust guests, were exorbitant, extravagant, and exceedingly wasteful; Jesus' kingdom feast, on the other hand, concluded with a concerted effort to collect all the leftovers. In a remarkable piece of instruction unique to John's Gospel, Jesus told his disciples to "[g]ather up the fragments left over, so that nothing may be lost" (6:12). God's kingdom seeks to gather up, to redeem, and to restore all things to health and plenteousness that nothing may be lost or wasted.

It is clear that children were among the throngs Jesus and his disciples served in these great messianic feasts, these foretastes of the coming reign of God. This should remind us that children, often marginalized and overlooked in Jesus' time, were special objects of his love and welcome. When his own disciples tried to put distance between themselves and bothersome little ones, Jesus scolded them, welcomed the children, and told his disciples "it is to such as these that the kingdom of heaven belongs" (Matt. 19:14).

God's Upside-Down Kingdom

No wonder John the Baptist felt confused! He preached the coming of a kingdom that would blaze forth in wrath, fire, and judgment (Matthew 3:7, 10-12), while Jesus offered forgiveness, healing, and grace. The Christian faith confesses that in Jesus, the kingdom of God is come. Jesus, in his teaching, mighty works, and humble love, embodies the actual reign of God. He is the Prince, heaven's Vanguard, the One who establishes a beachhead for the kingdom of heaven on earth. Thus, when a group of Pharisees quizzed Jesus about the date for the arrival of God's kingdom, he responded, "The kingdom of God is not coming with things that can be observed; nor will they say, 'Look, here it is!' or, 'There it is!' For, in fact, the kingdom of God is among you" (Luke 17:20-21). Recent biblical scholarship affirms that Jesus was referring to himself in this statement, revealing that he is the Representative of the Kingdom, the One in and by whom the kingdom of God had come.

Though the Kingdom was truly present in Jesus' ministry, there is also a future dimension to God's rule. In Luke's Gospel, we find a poignant portrait of Jesus' own anticipation of the future deliverance of all creation, set within the narrative of the last meal with his disciples. As Jesus ate and drank with his friends, he vowed not to partake again "until it is fulfilled in the kingdom of God," or "until the kingdom of God comes" (22:16, 18). Later that night, Jesus once more described God's rule as diametrically opposed to that of political potentates who lord their power over others. Simply stated, God is One who serves. This is the dimension of the Kingdom that is attainable in our lives today through the empowering presence of Christ the Servant among us (v. 27). But Jesus looked around the table and envisioned once more a future dimension of the Kingdom: "You are those who have stood by me in my trials; and I confer on you, just as my Father has conferred on me, a kingdom, so that you may eat and drink at my table in my kingdom, and you will sit on thrones judging the twelve tribes of Israel" (vv. 28-30).

So the kingdom of God is both present and future, holding us in the tension of "already/not yet." The rule of God is already here by the coming of Jesus and in Christ's continued presence through the gift of the Holy Spirit (Rom. 14:17); it is not yet in the sense that we await the fulfillment of the Kingdom in the messianic banquet and the healing of the nations.

Even so, Lord Jesus, come!

Reflect on this...

What are your thoughts and feelings after reading this chapter?

How has this chapter helped you better understand the Story of God?

In what ways are you involved in this part of God's Story today?

NOTES:

Other Dialog studies also available!

THE BEATITUDES
Living a Blessed Life

Discover why those who live as described in the Beatitudes are likely to find themselves both at odds with, and misunderstood by, cultures built on radically different assumptions.

PARTICIPANT'S GUIDE ISBN 978-0-8341-3374-7
FACILITATOR'S GUIDE ISBN 978-0-8341-3373-0

THE PROPHETS
Hearing the Timeless Voice of God

The prophets live during specific times and speak specific words to their listeners. Yet, because their messages are from God, their words are timeless. Learn about seven of these prophets, who they are, and the messages they deliver that transcend time to grow your spirit today.

PARTICIPANT'S GUIDE ISBN 978-0-8341-3376-1
FACILITATOR'S GUIDE ISBN 978-0-8341-3375-4

Available online at DialogSeries.com